The Barista reference book
Foundation

Complying with the programme Barista Skills Foundation

Author:
Alessandro Galtieri

SCA Member since 2005, AST since 2014
Content Creator – Brewing module
Owner of Aroma Bologna, advisor, trainer.

First English Edition May 2020

Photo credits:
Fotolia.com, Freepik.com, other pictures kindly provided by Chiara Bergonzi – drawn from the book LATTE ART published by Hoepli

Editor: Cristina Caroli
Graphics, illustrations and layout: Fabio Gamberini

Index

Chapter 1 - Coffee

Chapter 2 - Equipment

Chapter 3 - Espresso

Chapter 4 - Milk

Chapter 5 - Service Health Safety

CHAPTER 1
Coffee

Flavour:
term indicating the combination of taste and smell.

Variety features

Nowadays, almost all the coffee on the market belongs to two botanical varieties – the Arabica and the Canephora, better known as Robusta. These two varieties differ in various features, such as bean shape, size and colour, but also in their growing climates and altitudes, and in their resistance to parasites and diseases.

Let us see how the differences between the two varieties affect taste.

A Canephora espresso is characterised by a thick, brown crema with a coarse, sometimes rippled texture. Its body is dense, its taste strong, bitter, earthy and woody at times. Depending on its origin, it may develop flavours ranging from chocolaty to woody aromatic and spicy. Conversely, the Arabica espresso has a thin, elastic and persistent crema with a hazel-brown colour. Its body is syrupy but not mellow, clean and silky to the palate.

Its taste is dominated by a pleasant fruity acidity with citrus notes – ranging from lemon and grapefruit to mandarin and red orange.
Its aromatic structure is complex and articulated, and varies from fleshy fruit and flowers to wild berries and cocoa. It is also very persistent.

Below:
Coffee plant with ripening cherries

VARIETY FEATURES

ARABICA		ROBUSTA
MOUNTAINS	GROWING ENVIRONMENT	PLAIN
LOW	RESISTANCE TO PARASITES AND DISEASES	HIGH
LOW	CAFFEINE CONTENT	HIGH
FRUITY, FLOWERY, STRUCTURED	FLAVOURS	CHOCOLATY, DRIED FRUIT, ONE-DIMENSIONAL
BIG SIZE OVAL SHAPE CURVED CENTER CUT	BEAN FEATURES	SMALL SIZE ROUND SHAPE STRAIGHT CENTER CUT

FOCUS

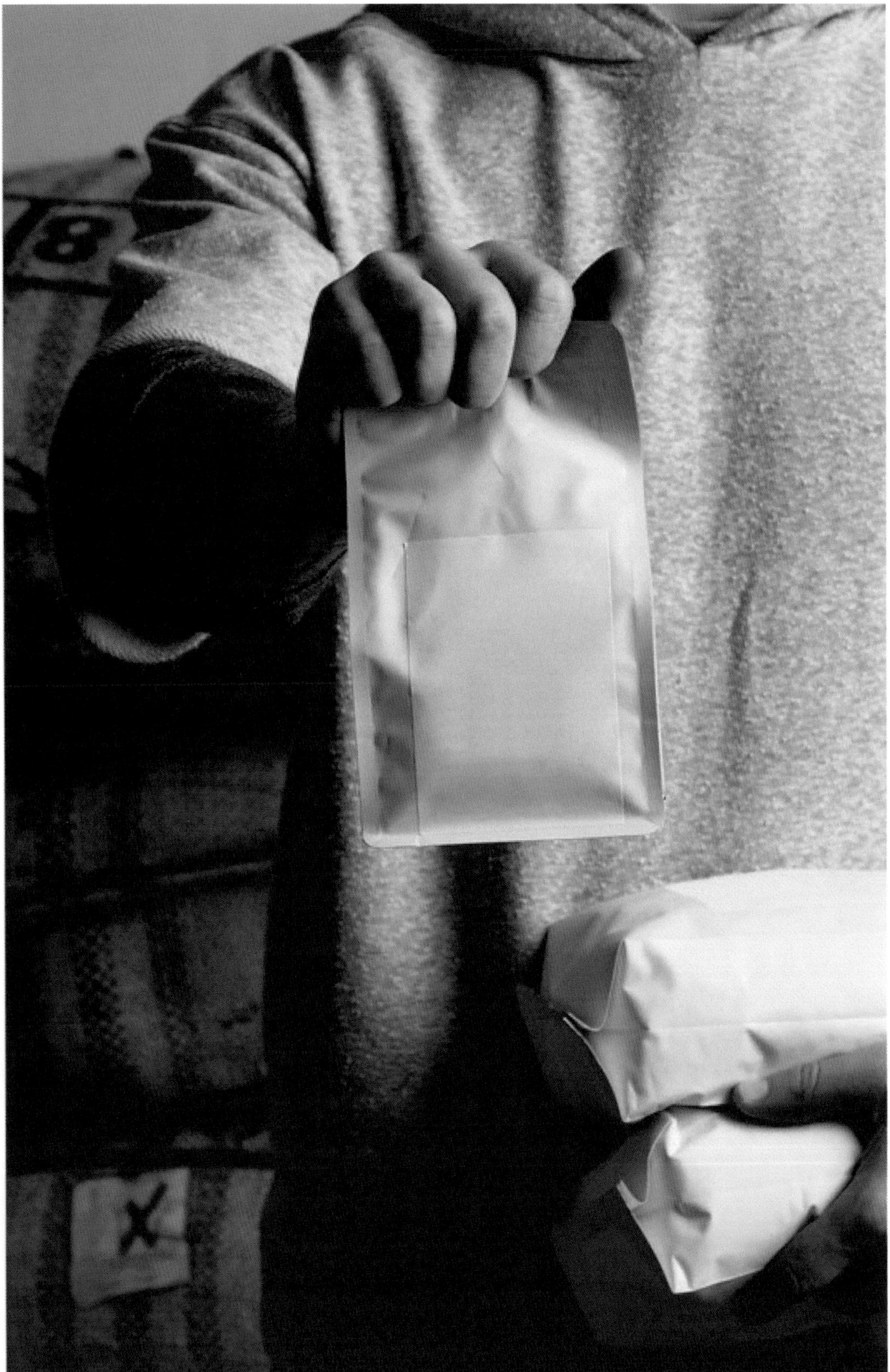

Ideally, roasted coffee should be consumed within one month and a half, three months at the most.

Preservation

Just like any other crop, coffee is subject to decay. In the producing Countries, after several selections and processing, beans are dried in order to decrease their percentage of moisture, thus ensuring longer preservation. This way, decay slows down but does not stop – this is why it is preferable to toast and use coffee within one year from its production. After this period, we should expect a sharp drop in the sensory features of the product. Roasted coffee decays faster than green coffee. The strong heat roasted coffee is exposed to and the subsequent physical-chemical changes it undergoes turn it into an extremely delicate product that is subject to rapid degeneration.

Also in this case – as we will see later –, there is something we can do to slow down its decay, but the degenerative process is inevitably a lot faster.

Even though the period of maximum sensory integrity of the pre-roast green coffee is one year, the ideal time range for the consumption of roasted coffee is one month – three months at the most for the best result in cup. After this period, the coffee will have completed its cycle of maximum vitality and will no longer provide the best results possible.

Even if these time limits are respected and all the necessary countermeasures are adopted, coffee will decay at any rate, so the sooner we consume it after its 'rest', the better results it will provide. When we talk about 'resting', we actually refer to 'degassing – 'i.e. a process that lasts a couple of days, during which the roasted beans lose the extra carbon dioxide that formed inside them during the roasting process.

From field to cup, coffee must be preserved in appropriate containers.

Once it has released the gas in excess, coffee starts its period of maximum fragrance and is ready to provide the best result in cup.

Air is the number one enemy of coffee, since it contains many elements that accelerate coffee degeneration

Coffee beans vs ground coffee

Roasters provide their professional customers with roasted coffee beans in sealed packages to best preserve the coffee from decay and external agents.

Coffee for professional use is sold in beans, while coffee for home use is usually ground – have you ever wondered why?

One of the main reasons why is the grind size of the coffee particles, which needs to be constantly calibrated and adjusted to obtain the best quality in cup.

This is because there is no standard coffee grinding size that suits any situation.

Another reason is that ground coffee exposes a greater surface to elements that determine its quick decay (oxygen, humidity, etc.).

Moreover, by breaking the bean structure we release and quickly disperse the aromas and volatile substances it contains.

Ultimately, the choice of keeping coffee in beans until it is used makes the Barista's work harder, but preserves the fragrance and quality of the drink – and that is a priority in coffeehouses.

At home, on the other hand, the priority for the consumer is ease of use, to the detriment of fragrance.

Once coffee is ground, its contact surface increase.

INCREASING COFFEE CONTACT SURFACE THROUGH GRINDING

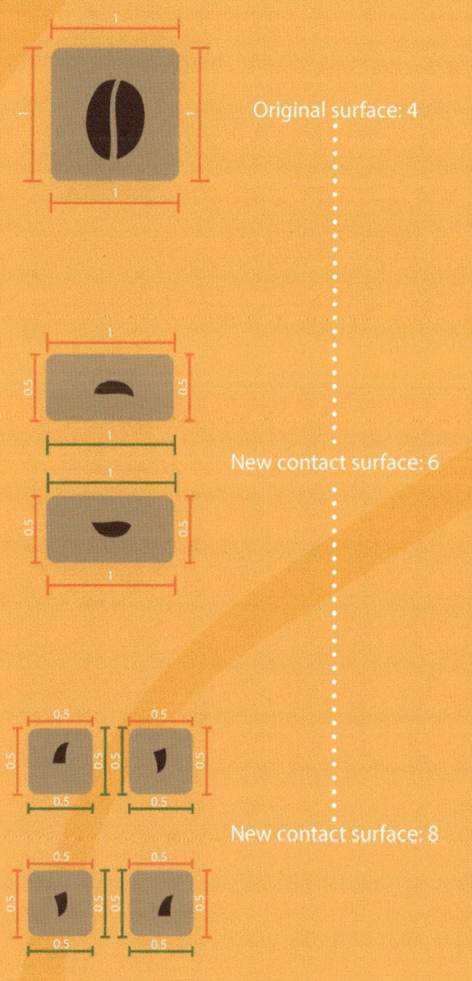

PIC. 1.4

THE SURFACE OF THE INTACT BEAN HAS A CERTAIN SIZE, MARKED IN RED.

WHEN THE BEAN IS CUT IN HALF, ITS SURFACE INCREASES – THE AREAS MARKED IN GREEN ADD UP.

IF THE TWO HALVES OBTAINED ARE CUT IN HALF, THE TOTAL SURFACE INCREASES AGAIN AND SO ON.

DESPITE THE ABSTRACT AND BIDIMENSIONAL PICTURE, IT IS EASY TO SEE HOW THE SMALLER THE GROUND COFFEE PARTICLES, THE LARGER ITS EXPOSED SURFACE.

New contact surface

Original contact surface

The Barista must preserve and store coffee in the most suited way to protect its sensory features as much as possible.

Why coffee decays quickly

One of the reasons is that during the roasting process, the coffee bean loses almost all the water it contains and becomes more porous and capillary. These two features make it particularly hygroscopic, i.e. capable of absorbing the water molecules in the atmosphere.

Another reason is that roasted coffee has a good percentage of fat substances, which can bind to oxygen molecules in the air very easily, thus producing the phenomenon of oxidation. This is rather harmful for the sensory notes of coffee, since it produces the same unpleasant rancid taste we can find, for example, in the fat of a slice of cheese that has been exposed to air for too long.

Air: Can indeed be considered the number one enemy of coffee, since it contains the elements that cause coffee decay and degeneration. What are these elements? Let us analyse them one by one and see how they affect coffee:

Humidity: There can be different percentages of humidity in the air, but usually this represents a relevant fraction of air composition. Humidity in the air is but 'micronized 'water floating just like the gases it is part of, thus becoming part of the atmosphere. When coffee is exposed to water molecules in the air, it absorbs them. This way, coffee becomes heavier, its physical properties change and it starts decaying faster.

Oxygen: It is responsible of the oxidation of fats in coffee. Some environmental conditions favour this bound between fats and oxygen – these are high temperature and intense light. The presence of these factors result in very fast oxidation and significant sensory damage.

Side.
By taking utmost care of coffee, the Barista contributes significantly to quality in cup.

MAIN CAUSES OF COFFEE DEGENERATION

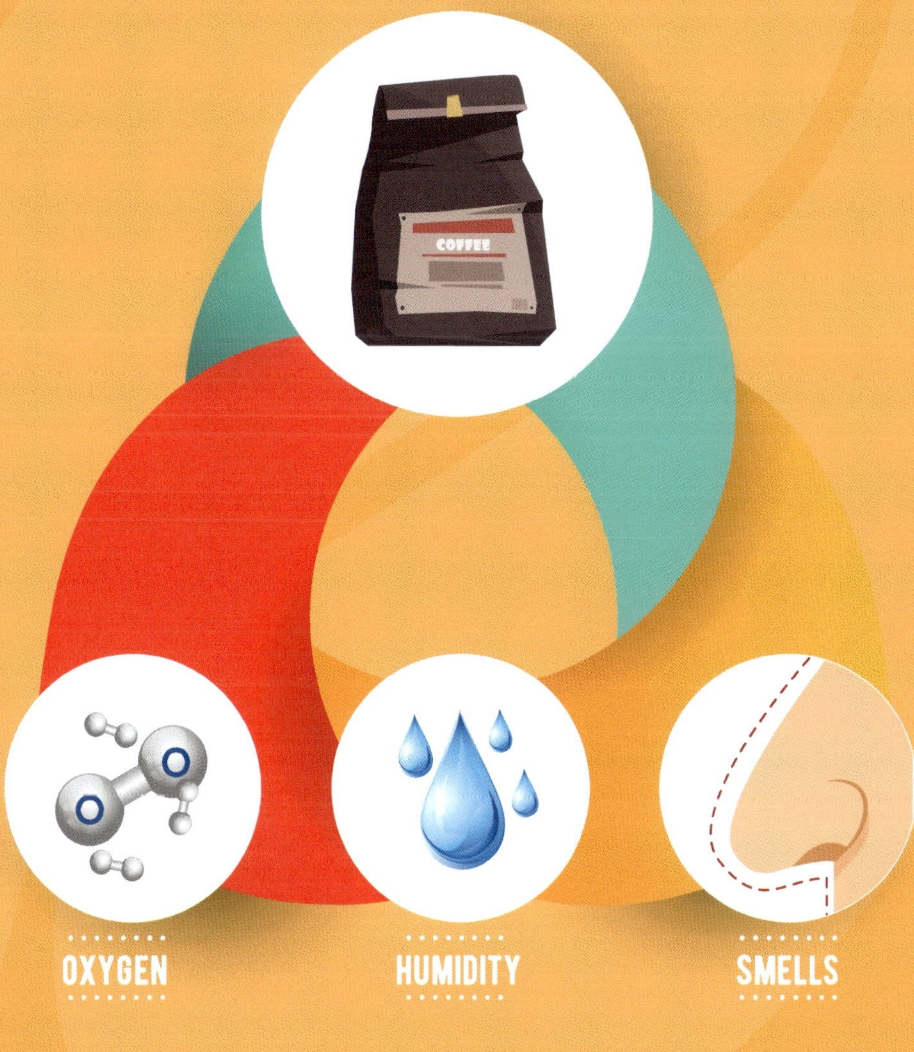

Coffee must be isolated from smells that can contaminate it.

Smells: Another effect of the properties of roasted coffee consists in absorbing and retaining smells from the air. Coffee absorbs smells very easily and retains them in its fats. Therefore, the Barista should work to preserve and store coffee in the most adequate way, protecting it from smell contamination, be it chemical or natural.

Airtight bags – manufactured with light and flexible, yet very effective materials – are the most common packages used in roasteries and provide the most effective barrier against harmful elements in the air.

Professionals must keep coffee in these packages and should take care not to damage them, for example by piercing them. The storage location must be fresh, dry, protected from intense light radiation and isolated from smells that could reach and contaminate coffee.

Air fresheners and detergents – often characterised by intense scents – but also food with strong smells should be kept away from it.

Preserving coffee quality in everyday use

Roasted coffee should be exposed to the air for the first time when it has to be used.

From now on, the oxidising processes accelerate and coffee must be brewed within a short time.

During this time, we need to pay proper attention to slow down the process, but also to brew coffee when its fragrance is still at its maximum.

Even though it might seem strange, the first operation to be carried out somehow contradicts what has been said so far: the coffee bag should be opened a few tens of minutes before using the coffee to make it 'breathe', just like red wine.

Just like it happens with certain wines, a brief and controlled oxidation makes the product best express its aromatic capacity, soften it on the palate and provides it with greater uniformity in sensory and extraction features.

Also, oxidation will make the beans at the bottom of the new bag more similar to those at the top, giving uniformity to the profile of the coffee in use.

The size of the bag should be calibrated with the amount of coffee consumed – the ideal solution would be consuming the whole bag in one day.

After the coffee has 'breathed', it must be poured into the hopper of the coffee grinder and the lid closed immediately to avoid further air exchange, which would accelerate oxidation.

A brief, controlled oxidation helps the product best express its aromatic capacity.

Coffee must be protected from the steam produced by the machine.

At the coffeehouse, milk-based drinks are prepared with the steam of the espresso machine, so the Barista should pay attention and prevent the coffee grinder from being exposed to a harmful cloud of steam every time they prepare a Cappuccino or an Espresso macchiato.

They must also pay attention to the position of the cup washer. As this produces heat and steam, they must not position it right underneath the coffee grinder.

At the end of the workday, the remaining beans must not be left in the hopper overnight. The Barista must pour them into a sealed airtight bag and store them where they can be preserved from oxidation.

IN BRIEF:

COFFEE

Must be consumed as freshly ground as possible.

Must be isolated from air with a suitable package.

Must be stored in a cool place,
away from direct light,
heat and strong smells.

Coffee in the grinder hopper must be used
within the workday,
while ground coffee
should be used immediately.

FOCUS

CHAPTER 2

Equipment

Coffee must be roasted and ground in order to be brewed – whatever the extraction method.

Coffee grinders

As we have already mentioned, roasteries provide coffeehouses with coffee in grains to best preserve its fragrance.

Coffee must be roasted and ground in order to be brewed – whatever the extraction method. The espresso method is not an exception.

The device most commonly used for this operation is the doser-grinder.

This piece of equipment has cutting burrs that grind the coffee beans into very fine particles that are collected into a built-in cylindrical container.

The container is equipped with a volumetric doser that provides the desired dose of ground coffee when a lever is pulled.

More recently, an alternative to the doser-grinder has been developed – the on-demand grinder.

The difference between the two devices lies in the dosing mechanism; apart from this, as far as grinding is concerned, they are identical.

The volumetric doser consists in a separator that divides the lower part of the container into sectors the height of which can be adjusted by turning a screw.

By modifying the height of the sectors their volume changes and so does the dose of ground coffee they contain.
On-demand grinders are not equipped with a container-doser, so the ground coffee falls directly into the filter that is right outside the grinding chamber. In this case, an adjustable timer provides the doses. By grinding the coffee for a shorter or longer time, you will obtain a larger or smaller dose.

The reason why this new device was introduced is that often ground coffee remains in the doser-grinder for a long time and this has to be avoided as much as possible to prevent a rapid decay of the aromatic properties of coffee.

The on-demand grinder has the advantage of providing a freshly ground coffee powder characterised by a greater fragrance and taste potential in cup.

Left:
Always place the lid onto the hopper.

Many beginners mistakenly focus their attention on the espresso machine, considering the grinder a minor device.

Adjusting the coffee grinder

Many beginners mistakenly focus their attention on the espresso machine, considering the grinder a minor device. In fact, its function is essential.

This is the device the user interacts with most often to adjust the ground coffee fineness – the grind, in technical terms – and the dose so that the coffee cake offers the right resistance to the passage of high-pressure hot water from the espresso machine.

The first thing to do when we start working with a new grinder is reading its instructions. With a good knowledge of the parts and software of these electronic devices, we can get familiar with them more easily and quickly, thus avoiding troubles.

The coffee grinder adjustment starts with searching for the right grind. If the device is completely out of calibration, you need to find a point of reference.

Move the burrs closer together until they touch, then move them apart of a couple of markings.

From this point – very close to zero – move the burrs apart of an arbitrary gap, for example 4 or 5 markings.

Pour the beans into the hopper and open the shutter.

Grind a couple of doses, pour a two-cup dose and brew the Espressos – check if the time and volume parameters are respected.

If the brewing time of the set volume is too short, the burrs should be moved closer together; if it is too long, they should be moved apart.
Once the gap between burrs has been changed, grind a certain amount of coffee and throw it away in order to remove all the coffee of the previous grinding from the grinding chamber and the collector.

The coffee grinder adjustment starts with searching for the right grind. If the device is completely out of calibration, you need to find a point of reference.

Grind another dose and try again until you reach the desired parameters.

To adjust the dose in doser-grinders, grind a certain amount of coffee to fill the dosing chamber for approximately half of its volume. Take two doses by pulling the dosing lever and letting it snap back with the return spring (do not guide it with your hand) and using a tenth of a gram scale.

If the dose is scarce, lift the doser top with the adjustment screw, as shown in the instructions. If it is abundant, lower it.

In on-demand grinders, the grinding time calibrates the dose. Set an arbitrary grinding time – for example 3.5 seconds for the double dose –, then grind and weigh the coffee. If the dose is scarce, set a longer time. If it is abundant, set a shorter time.

On-demand grinders with gravimetric dosing have been launched on the market recently but are not yet widely used. They are equipped with a system that measures the dose weight directly.

Below.
Adjust the grind by turning the adjustment screw.

ON DEMAND GRINDER

A: LID
B: HOPPER
C: SHUTTER
D: GRIND ADJUSTMENT SCREW
E: DISPLAY
F: GRINDING TIME BUTTONS
G: GROUND COFFEE OUTLET
H: PORTAFILTER SUPPORT FORK
I: RESIDUE TRAY

DOSER/ GRINDER

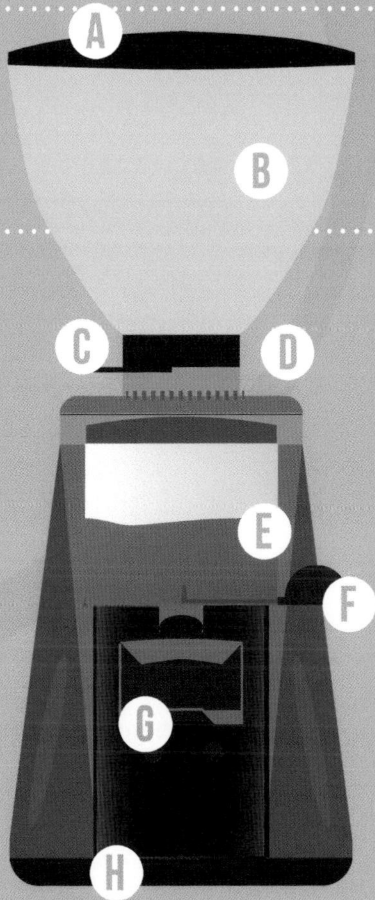

A: LID
B: HOPPER
C: SHUTTER
D: GRIND ADJUSTMENT SCREW
E: DOSER
F: DOSING LEVER
G: PORTAFILTER SUPPORT FORK
H: RESIDUE TRAY

"The value of an espresso machine shall be measured by its capacity to keep its temperature constant."

The espresso machine

The traditional espresso machine here described contains a boiler made of a sealed, usually horizontal metal cylinder that is 2/3 full of water.

Inside the boiler are one or more electric heaters. Generally, water temperature within the boiler is kept at around 120°C.

This measurement is not shown – you need to deduce it from the boiler pressure shown by the pressure gauge on the front of the machine. The correct pressure value is 1 – 1.1 BAR (acceptable range 1 – 1.5 BAR).

In the models equipped with a volumetric pump – also known as 'free-flow machines' –, another pressure gauge shows the brewing pressure, i.e. the pressure at which water is pushed through the coffee cake. This is usually 9 BAR, but in variable pressure machines it ranges from 7 to 11 BAR.

In the most popular models, water reaches a pre-infusion chamber inside the brew group when the brew control is pressed.

From here, the shower distributes water evenly and delicately, soaking the coffee cake before pressure increases and the water hits the cake with all its extracting power.

This easy operation is very important because it prepares the coffee for the best extraction. It expands the volume of the coffee cake and compacts it in its gaps so that it can resist the force of the water column that will flow through it in few seconds.
Moreover, it solubilises the water-soluble substances and protects the proteins from a shock that might damage them with a subsequent negative effect on the creaminess of the espresso.

THE ESPRESSO MACHINE

A: CUP WARMING TRAY
B: KNOBS/LEVER FOR STEAM SUPPLY
C: KNOB/LEVER FOR THE SUPPLY OF WATER FROM BOILER

D: HOT WATER DISPENSER
E: STEAM WANDS
F: BREW GROUP
G: PORTAFILTER

H: SPOUTS
I: PRESSURE GAUGES
L: DRIP TRAY

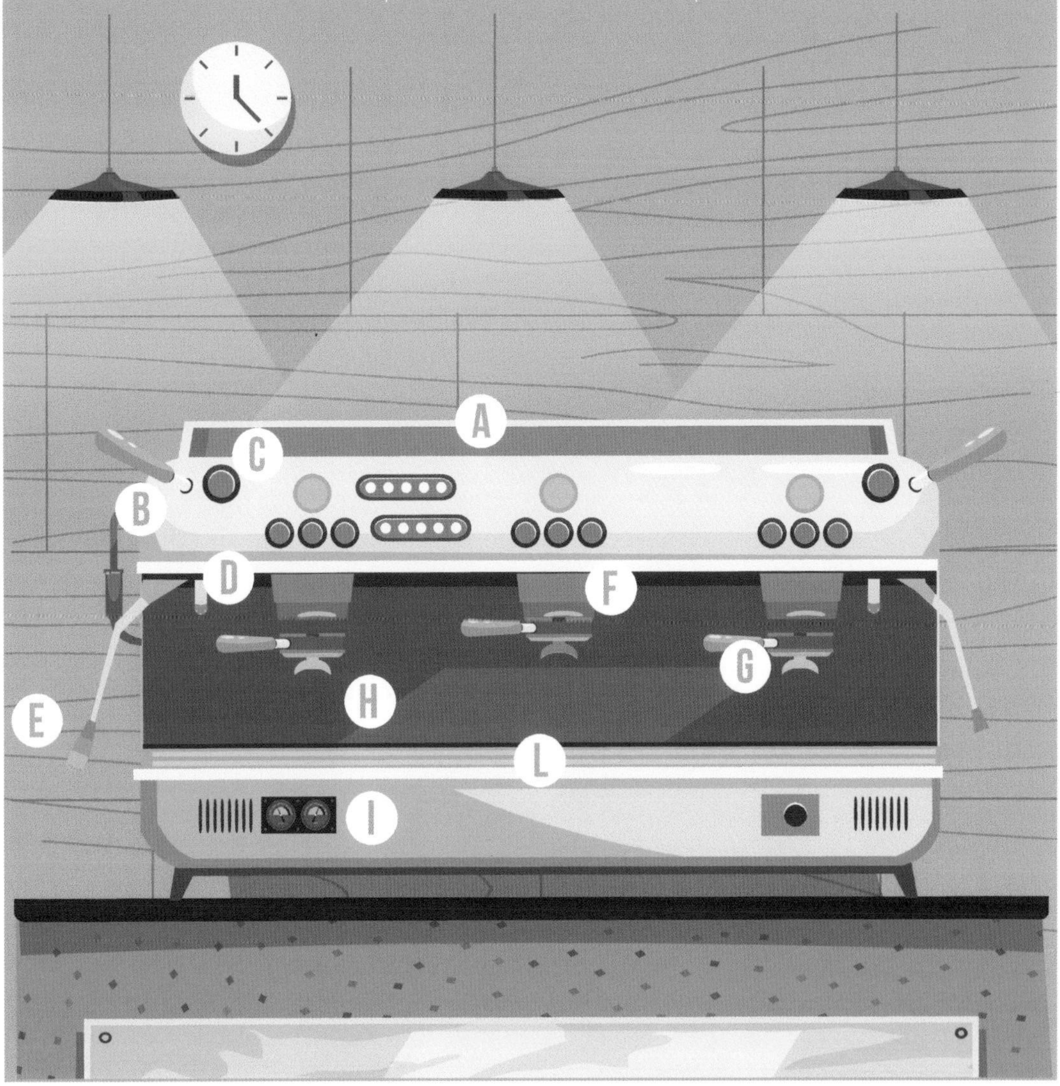

Remember:
1 bar = 120°C
1,2 bar = 123°C

Filters play a relevant function as well – their perfect geometry allows a better exploitation of the coffee cake.

Portafilters act as filter basket housings and brew group attachments, and distribute the drink into cups through their spouts.

Other parts of the espresso machine are:

A cup warming tray to keep the cups warm and dry.

A tap linked to a pipe that collects steam from the upper part of the boiler and conveys it into the steam wands – bended pipes with a jet terminal with calibrated and oriented holes for correct milk frothing.

A tap connected to a pipe that collects hot water from the bottom of the boiler.

A pressure sensor inside the boiler provides data on internal pressure.

A pressure gauge showing the pressure from which we can deduce the temperature of water in the boiler (1 BAR = 120°C – 1.2 BAR = 123°C).
Another pressure gauge showing the delivery pressure.

A non-return valve that prevents fluids from entering the boiler after a depression produced in the boiler itself before the right pressure is reached.

A safety valve, just like in all pressure devices.

The correct pressure value is 1 – 1.1 BAR (acceptable range 1 – 1.5 BAR).

Water treatment

Usually water contains too much calcium and this could build up as limescale on the heating elements.

Water from the water system usually contains too much calcium and magnesium, which could build up as limescale on the heating parts of the boiler, as it happens in common washing machines.

However, while in a washing machine we can solve the problem with anti-limescale products, we cannot do the same with an espresso machine. We can reduce or remove limescale in water by means of several devices or using different treatments: the water softener, the filter cartridge and reverse osmosis.

The water softener turns all the calcium and magnesium into sodium, which does not produce limescale, the filter cartridge lowers the calcium and magnesium content by turning it into hydrogen, while reverse osmosis forces water through a molecular or atomic membrane producing demineralised water.

Water from the water network also contains substances that bind to coffee, affecting its chemical and sensory properties.

One of these is chlorine, present in all aqueducts. Therefore, water treatment should remove this substance as well.

The espresso cup

Every drink has its own ideal container to enhance its properties.

As consumers, we usually drink the espresso in the typical small cup with features that make it perfect for this drink.

In search of distinctive elements, some Baristas make unintentional mistakes by using cups that differ in shape, capacity, size and materials. The ideal container for tasting the espresso is a cup with a capacity of 60-90 ml, made of a material with good thermal inertia to preserve the heat accumulated on the cup warming tray and with a rim that is thin enough to make the act of drinking easy and to convey a sense of fineness.

In addition, ease of use is particularly relevant, as well as mechanical resistance to the work pace during peak times at the coffeehouse. The colour on the inside of the cup is white and even to allow a correct perception of the colour of the crema. The material that best meets these requirements is porcelain.

Geometry is also essential – the internal bottom of the cup must be curve, free from edges and angles to let the crema emulsion surface easily. Moreover, the diameter of the rim should be the result of a compromise between preventing the crema from dispersing in too wide a surface and letting the taster's nose into the cup so that they can enjoy the smell and taste the coffee more comfortably.

IN BRIEF:

GRINDING

Fill the hopper.

Grind a dose of coffee to operate the burrs, then remove it.

Grind and weigh the requested dose.

Adjust the dose, if necessary.

Extract the espresso and check if the requested volume is brewed in the correct time.

Adjust the grind to fix the extraction time, if necessary.

FOCUS

CHAPTER 3

Espresso

The great energy provided by pressure adds up to the thermal energy provided by water.

What is Espresso?

The espresso coffee results from the percolation of high-pressure hot water through a cake of roasted, ground and compressed coffee in calibrated times and volumes. The resulting drink is rich in dissolved soluble substances and insoluble substances that have been dragged through a metal filter and into the cup.

One of the main distinctive features of the espresso is the crema floating on the drink, produced by the energy provided by water pressure and heat.

This big energy supply allows coffee to be strongly concentrated and correctly exploited in a very short time.

The drink is made of different layers. On its surface is the crema – a micro-foam of colloidal substances, micro-particles of insoluble substances and polymers. Due to water pressure, these substances trap tiny air bubbles and produce the foam.

Below the crema is an invisible but very important layer of oil, which provides essential aromas and acts as a support for the overlying crema.

Finally, there is a water solution – the actual drink – made of sugars, acids, proteins, phenolic substances and caffeine, where further gas bubble and solids are dispersed.

This complex and precious structure exalts the aromatic properties of the espresso, since the crema on the surface releases the volatile substances of the hot, freshly brewed drink into the environment, towards the taster's nose.

The layer of crema also retains part of the aromatic content in the liquid below, thus ensuring that the aromatic content is released gradually and preserved for the actual tasting.

IN BRIEF

CORRECT EXTRACTION

OVER-EXTRACTED

UNDER-EXTRACTED

FOCUS

The crema is an instable structure, destined to dissolve in a short time.

However, the crema is an instable structure, destined to dissolve in a short time. In order to taste it at its best, therefore, the taster must drink the espresso as soon as it is prepared.

The type of coffee used, its freshness, roast and sugar content plays an essential role in foam stabilisation.

Espresso preparation

Distribute the dose evenly in the filter to avoid creating areas of higher or lower density.

More or less everyone has brewed coffee in their lives. This make some people think that it is an easy operation that does not need any in-depth study. To brew an espresso professionally, nevertheless, the Barista must follow a set of procedures and methods that have been developed and codified by the world of competitions, where the best professionals in the sector show their skills and the judges, with their strict selections, contribute to raise the level of the techniques used year after year.

Let's go deep in the details.

First, make sure that the hopper of the coffee grinder contains an adequate quantity of coffee beans and that the doser sections – in the models that come with this feature – are completely full of ground coffee.

Check that the parameters of the espresso machine are correct, the pressure of water of 9 BAR, the pressure in the boiler of 1.0 – 1.1 BAR. Make sure that portafilters are warm, that there are cups on the cup warming

"In order to distribute and level the coffee evenly you must not tap with the tamper".

tray and that every piece of equipment and accessory needed for the service (milk pitcher, dishes and coffee spoons) is in place and at hand.

Unlock the portafilter from the group head and flush a small amount of water from the shower to rinse it.

Remove the exhausted coffee cake accurately, then clean and dry filter and spouts with a special dry cloth.

Take the right dose of ground coffee, make sure that no coffee grinds are dispersed and distribute the dose evenly in the filter to avoid creating areas of higher or lower density.

During the espresso shot, this unevenness would cause the phenomenon of channelling, i.e. the creation of preferential pathways water would flow through, thus avoiding other parts of the cake.

In order to distribute and level the coffee evenly, you must not tap with the tamper.

Place the portafilter onto a solid surface and prepare to compress the coffee by placing the handheld tamper perpendicular to the filter bottom.

Tamp the coffee with a precise and uniform movement, taking care to preserve the planarity of the cake surface, until the tamper stops, meaning that compression is completed.

Make sure the portafilter is placed on a stable surface at the right height when compressing the cake to preserve your muscles and joints from strains.

Remove any possible coffee grinds from the rim of the filter with the palm of your hand, then use thumb and finger to clean the portafilter bayonet lock.

Clean and dry the drip tray grid with another cloth, lock the portafilter into the group head – make sure not to damage the compressed cake by hitting the portafilter against the group head or the drip tray.

CHANNELING

Start the shot immediately – never let the coffee wait in the portafilter that has already been locked into the group head – and place the cup onto the drip tray grid right under the spouts.

If there are no further coffee shots to make, unlock the portafilter, flush, remove the coffee cake from the filter and lock the portafilter back into the group head after cleaning and drying the filter. Clean the drip tray grid with a cloth.

The espresso is the result of a play of antagonist forces that must be kept in balance.

There are many variables that must be kept under control.

Choosing this balance – just like choosing doses and times – requires a certain knowledge and familiarity with product and equipment. This is why we are not dealing with it in this book – we will rely on the trainer or roaster's parameters, making sure they do not change over time.

If you follow these parameters, you will exclude most of the variables and you will be able to focus on the only adjustment you are responsible of – the grind.

Often, when we ask for suggestions on how to use a blend, we only get data on the dose. The remaining information – including the amount of liquid and crema in the cup – is taken for granted.

Even though you might argue that it is widely known that the crema fills half of the cup, "half of the cup" is a very imprecise measure and there can be big differences in the thickness of the crema among different coffees, but also among the different ripeness degrees of the same coffee.

For this reason, it is advisable to use transparent graduated doser glasses in order to assess the volume of coffee with consistency and precision during grind assessment and adjustment.

The espresso dose is usually 7 grams per cup, but it is often advisable to use a larger dose.

Side:
Pressurised water tends to find pathways of least resistance to flow through in the coffee cake, so the tamper must be perpendicular and flat when pressing the coffee to avoid the phenomenon of "channelling"..

Moreover, transparency lets you focus on the liquid and exclude the crema, thus obtaining information that is more reliable.

The dose of the espresso usually amounts to 7 grams per cup.

However, this value is not fixed, since many roasters suggest using larger doses for their products. The dose must be consistent throughout the shots, since it determines a higher or lower resistance to the water flow and this affects the brewing time.

The volume in cup depends on the dose and the coffee delivery time can range from 20 to 30 seconds.

Suppose you have received the following coffee brewing recipe from the roaster.

Dose of 14 grams for double filter

Yield in the cup: 30 ml

Time: 25 seconds

Brew the double espresso into the graduated glass and assess how long it takes to obtain that volume of liquid (excluding the crema).

If the extraction time is 25 seconds, the adjustment is perfect and this will result in a full body, a good balance of flavours and a nice, persistent crema.

THE ESPRESSO SEQUENCE

1. Unlock the portafilter
2. Flush briefly
3. Clean the drip tray grid with the special cloth
4. Gently tap the portafilter on the knock-out drawer to remove the exhausted coffee cake
5. Clean and dry the spouts
6. Remove ground coffee residues from the filter with a dry cloth
7. Pour the coffee dose
8. Distribute the ground coffee
9. Place the portafilter on a stable surface, at the right height
10. Place the tamper onto the ground coffee, making sure it is perpendicular
11. Tamp without excesses to obtain a flat, compact and uniform surface
12. Remove coffee grinds from the rim of the filter and from the portafilter lock
13. Lock the portafilter into the group head making sure it does not hit the machine and start the shot immediately
14. Place the cups under the spouts, holding them by their handles, before the coffee starts flowing out

1
2
3
4
5
6
1 2 C
7
8
9
10
90°
11
12
13
14

Grinding has a crucial effect on extraction, as it can affect the process significantly.

Should you obtain the same volume in 15 seconds, for example, you would have an under-extracted – i.e. underexploited – espresso.

Apart from the quick flow of water through the coffee cake, the under-extraction features are: a very light body, a sour, unbalanced taste and a crema that is light in colour.

In order to deal with this extraction defect, a finer grind should be set.

Should you obtain that same volume in 35 seconds, on the other hand, the espresso would be over-exploited, i.e. over-extracted.

An over-extracted espresso is characterised by a very slow flow of liquid from the shower, a bitter taste and a dark crema with a lighter spot where the liquid lands.If the espresso has these characteristics, the Barista needs to set a coarser grind to decrease coffee resistance to the water flow.

Once you have found the right balance, your work is not over yet. Small changes depending on environmental conditions – such as temperature and humidity, different degrees of ripeness of the beans, burr wear and overheating – affect the grind, so you need to make micro-adjustments to keep the desired parameters consistent.

SCA COFFEE BREWING PARAMETERS

	SINGLE	DOUBLE
DOSE	7-10G.	14-20G.
BEVERAGE WEIGHT	10,5-25G.	21-50G.
TIME	20-30″	20-30″
BREW FORMULA	1:1.5-1:2.5	1:1.5-1:2.5

Coffee grinding

> **Once you have found the sweet spot, you need to keep it by means of frequent micro-adjustments.**

In order to be brewed, coffee must be ground. Grinding makes the coffee release its precious load of tastes and smells. When the beans are turned into small particles, a larger coffee surface is exposed to water, so a greater amount of aromatic molecules will be reached and dragged into the cup in the same time interval.

Without grinding, water could not solubilise the inner cells of coffee and this would therefore prevent us from to enjoying the sensory potential of the product at its full. The effect of grinding on extraction is therefore essential and can affect the process significantly. A correct calibration of the grind allows the Barista to obtain the best possible result in terms of body and aromas.

An increased coffee surface, on the other hand, leads to a quick loss of volatile substances and exposes coffee to oxygen, which will spoil it rapidly.

This is why this operation needs to be carried out only when brewing the coffee. For this reason, on-demand grinders are excellent for providing the Barista with freshly ground, fragrant coffee.

IN BRIEF:

EXTRACTION VARIABLES

Coffee dose

Water temperature

Extraction time

Coffee dose – water volume ratio

Pump pressure

Grind

Ground coffee distribution

Tamping

FOCUS

CAPITOLO 4

Milk

It is important to be able to rely on efficient refrigerators, with a controlled temperature of +4°C.

Milk knowledge

Milk is the second most important ingredient in a coffeehouse after coffee. Milk is used to produce the most typical, renowned and appreciated drink of the Italian breakfast – the Cappuccino.

Due to the importance of this drink, it is essential for the professional barista to know and use coffee at its best. When we talk about milk, we refer to the cow milk.

By Italian laws, the label on a container of milk produced by other mammals must specify the animal it was milked from. If it is not specified, it is implied it is dairy. Nowadays, there are many types of milk on the market, but the most suited for the preparation of a traditional Cappuccino is fresh, whole milk with the 3.2% of proteins and the 3.6% of fats.

Fresh whole milk is richer in nutrients and has a more complete taste than other milks because it is intact in its natural composition, it is freshly milked and the hygiene treatments it undergoes are calibrated to alter its properties as little as possible.

Side.
It is advisable to have pitchers of different sizes to adjust the quantity of milk to froth and avoid waste.

THE CLASSIC CAPPUCCINO

"MONK'S HEAD"

Milk micro foam

Milk and coffee

Coffee

Ceramic

Milk is a delicate, highly perishable product. In certain conditions, microorganisms can easily attack it and find in it a nutritious environment where to build their undesired colonies. Therefore, all the necessary measures must be taken to preserve its freshness.

The more time passes from milking, the more the milk can be affected, so the easiest way to avoid problems is to use freshly milked milk. As time passes, milk can also lose its capacity of incorporating air. This is another reason for buying always freshly produced milk. Of course, expired milk will never be used and will be thrown away due to safety reasons.

It is important to be able to rely on efficient fridges, with a controlled temperature of +4°C. It is also advisable to have pitchers of different sizes to adjust the quantity of milk to be heated and avoid waste.

Milk preservation should be given the greatest attention in order to avoid milk decay. The biology of microorganisms can be dramatically slowed down if milk is preserved at a low temperature, so it is important to have efficient refrigerators with controlled temperature.

Storing and usage methods are also important – such as ensuring a correct milk turnover by placing the fresher milk behind the older one and keeping the milk outside the fridge for as little as possible.

Avoid leaving used pitches with milk traces waiting to be used again. Rinse and drain the pitches to avoid creating a microbe-friendly environment that would contaminate the new milk. Clean the steam wand thoroughly after every use with a clean, damp cloth.

Ensure correct milk turnover in the fridge by placing the fresher milk behind the older milk.

Milk deteriorates dramatically also when it is subject to high temperatures – that is why it must never exceed the temperature of 70°C during frothing.
The drink must fill the cup almost up to its rim and the crema must be 1-1.5 cm thick.

You must properly froth milk to obtain a creamy foam with micro-bubbles.

The espresso machine provides a particular form of milk heating that produces a layer of foam.

The Cappuccino

Ever since the 17th Century, many drinks based on coffee and milk have been experimented in western Countries. The most typical Italian coffee-based drink is the Cappuccino – a unique drink with specific features.

The Cappuccino comes from Italy and dates back to the invention and evolution of the espresso machine in the mid-20th Century, when a new heating method allowed to produce a layer of foam.

Contemporarily, that same machine produced a particularly concentrated coffee drink with a foamy emulsion on its surface – the Espresso coffee.

Over time, with practice and equipment evolution, these two ingredients found a balance in the proportions, extraction technique, temperature and process and we are now able to codify its features.

The Cappuccino is made with an Espresso brewed and poured into a hot porcelain cup with a capacity of 150-200 ml.

110-150 grams of milk must be frothed at a temperature that ranges from 50 to 70°C – with an ideal interval between 55 and 65°C – to obtain a creamy foam with micro-bubbles. The milk must be poured with an adequate technique to produce an abundant milk-white surface in the centre, circled by a thin brown ring provided by the coffee crema.

The creamy foam must be 1-1.5 cm thick, the espresso must be brewed with the same proportions used for the small cup, the fresh whole milk must be frothed starting from a temperature of 4°C, the cup must be filled up to the rim.

The most suited pitcher for milk frothing has well-defined features, particularly if you use it for Latte Art.

As far as geometry is concerned, the pitcher must have a larger bottom and a narrower mouth to prevent milk from spilling during frothing.

The material must be resistant to impacts and thermal shocks; it must be able to pass from cold to hot temperatures without consequences and it must be easily washable.

Professionals usually choose thick steel – the material that best meets these requirements. Baristas – especially beginners – should try to use cooled down pitchers (rinsed with water and accurately drained) in order to manage the rise of temperature in milk during frothing.

A temperature that is just a few degrees lower can make the difference, especially for an inexpert Barista.

The pitcher should have a handle for a firm, steady grip and a spout for a precise control when pouring the milk-foam mixture.

The pitcher must be filled half full to prevent the liquid from overflowing during frothing, when the formation of foam increases its volume.

The Barista should be equipped with pitchers of different sizes to calibrate the quantity of milk to be heated and avoid waste.

A product that has already been stressed and diluted by previous frothing would not be suitable for the preparation of a Cappuccino.

With pitchers of different sizes, the Barista can froth only the necessary quantity of milk, thus eliminating the problem of reusing a stressed, diluted milk.

Another essential element in Cappuccino preparation is the steam supplied by the boiler of the espresso machine, so also steam must have the right features for a perfect result.

A pressure of 1 BAR in boiler corresponds to a temperature of approximately 120°C.

Milk frothing:

1. Fill the pitcher half full.

2. Remove water condensation by purging – i.e. releasing the steam.

3. Dip the steam wand jet approximately 1 cm into the milk and release the steam at maximum power.

4. Inject air into the milk for a few seconds, until it reaches the temperature of your hand.

5. When the milk reaches a temperature of approximately 60°C, create a vortex without incorporating more air and stop the steam flow.

6. Clean the steam wand accurately immediately after use.

7. Purge to remove any possible milk traces from the internal part of the wand.

MILK FROTHING

After cleaning the steam wand, start swirling the pitcher horizontally to mix the hot liquid with the overlying foam

Turn on the steam tap with your left hand, making sure the pitcher is perfectly still in the right position, then let go of the tap e touch the side of the pitcher to feel its temperature. Air is injected into the liquid in these first seconds.

At the end of this first frothing stage, the air trapped in the milk will increase the milk volume and the jet will be completely immersed.

Make sure that this phase takes place before the milk reaches the temperature of your hand (approx. 37°C).

From now on, you must no longer inject air, but rather process the air that has already been trapped in big bubbles by positioning the steam wand so that it impresses a circular, horizontal movement to the milk – the so-called vortex. At this stage, air bubbles break up into smaller bubbles until they become microscopic and give the foam a smooth, creamy texture.

When your left hand feels the heat has reached an unpleasant level and starts burning, keep the pitcher still and turn off the steam tap. Since everyone has a different sensitivity to heat, it is advisable to use an immersion thermometer in order to be more precise in evaluating the final temperature, always keeping in mind that there is a delay in the display of the actual temperature. So, basically, if you want to reach a final temperature of 60°C you must turn off the steam tap when the thermometer shows 50°C. Keep still in this position for an instant to ensure the steam flow is completely over and then remove the pitcher by placing it onto a stable work surface. If the barista is left-handed, invert the positioning and use of hands.

Swirl the pitcher horizontally to evenly mix milk and foam to obtain a uniform, glossy and liquid surface.

If the customer asks you for a larger quantity of foam, you need to slide the pitcher downwards slowly and progressively in the first frothing phase, until the liquid reaches the temperature of your hand, so that more air is injected.

Milk pouring technique

After cleaning the steam wand, start swirling the pitcher horizontally to mix the hot liquid with the overlying foam.

Continue with this movement until you obtain an even, dense surface that is free from big bubbles, humid and brilliant, and follows the movement of the pitcher during its swirling.

This operation must be repeated every time before pouring the milk.

Now you are ready to pour the milk onto the espresso.

In case the amount of frothed milk is destined to more than one Cappuccino – for example two – you need to distribute the foam correctly between the two drinks.

If you poured the milk without taking any measures, you would obtain one Cappuccino with too much foam and another one with too little.

In order to avoid this inconvenience, mix milk and foam, then pour part of the liquid in a second pitcher.

The first cappuccino is prepared using the milk poured into the second pitcher , always swirling the pitcher horizontally to mix the hot liquid with the overlying foam.

Turn to mix again the liquid left in the first pitcher, gently pour it into the second, and make the second cappuccino, thus obtaining a correct distribution of the cream.

To obtain a good contrast of colours and a correct proportion of the shapes, it is necessary to pour the milk by placing the milk spout on the surface of the coffee with the cup tilted, pouring at a distance of about 10 cm, with the intent of making the cream arrive of milk under the surface of the espresso, piercing it.

THE POURING SEQUENCE

1. After frothing, swirl the pitcher horizontally to evenly mix the milk and foam, then pour.

2. Keep the pitcher far enough from the cup when pouring to make the milk foam pass under the surface of coffee

3. Move the pitcher closer to the cup when pouring to create a contrast in colours

COMMON MISTAKES TO AVOID DURING FROTHING:

Filling the pitcher with too much or too little milk compared to pitcher capacity.

Positioning the wand terminal too deep or too shallow into the milk in the first phase

Lifting and lowering the pitcher

Moving the pitcher forward or backward

Swirling the pitcher horizontally

Letting the steam wand touch the metal of the pitcher

Positioning the wand terminal too shallow into the milk in the second phase.

By subsequently bringing the pitcher spout to the surface, a white circle will be created in stark contrast to the brown color of the coffee cream, creating the thin crown, typical of traditional cappuccino.

If necessary, it is possible to increase the milk cream spill by raising the bottom of the pitcher, giving a slight horizontal wave movement left/right.

Without a correct milk pouring technique it is impossible to make a cappuccino with the characteristics described.

With an incorrect technique, a completely white or beige surface is obtained.

IN BRIEF:

THE MILK DOES NOT FROTH

Expired or not fresh milk

Mistakes in frothing technique

Obstruction of holes in the steam wand jet

Insufficient boiler pressure

Previously frothed milk

FOCUS

CHAPTER 5

Service Health Safety

DAILY CLEANING OF THE COFFEE GRINDER

- Close the hopper shutter and remove it from the body of the coffee grinder.
- Remove all the beans you can reach from the grinder.
- Pour the beans from the hopper into the airtight bag, remove all the air from the bag, then seal it and store it properly.
- Remove the oil and smell traces from the hopper with water and soap or with a detergent.
- Dry the surfaces completely, removing any trace of humidity.
- Operate the burrs to remove all the beans from the grinding chamber.
- Clean the burrs and the grinding chamber at least once a week with grinder cleaning pellets.
- In doser-grinders, remove the grounds with a brush.
- Remove the oil residues from the internal surfaces of the doser with a specific fragrance-free detergent and paper towel.
- Clean the coffee residues from residue tray and chassis.
- Clean the hopper with a fragrance-free detergent on a daily base.

DAILY CLEANING OF THE ESPRESSO MACHINE

- Clean the gasket with the special brush and remember to remove the grinds from the bayonet lock slots of the brew group.
- Clean the shower with a cloth.
- Put a blind filter in the portafilter and pour a dose of detergent into it.
- Lock the portafilter in and turn the water group ON for back-flushing. After 8-10 seconds, turn the flow off.
- Wait for 8-10 seconds to let the detergent clean the pipes and repeat the operation for a few times until the water flowing out is clean.
- Carry out this operation for every group head.
- Wear protective gloves, flush water from each group head into the unlocked blind filter until it is full, move it closer and than further away from the group head until water overflows to rinse the lock notches.
- Pour hot water and a dose of detergent into a vessel.
- Soak filters and portafilters in it for 10-15 minutes. Rinse carefully
- Put the filters back in the portafilters, checking the filter attachment spring is in position.
- Lock the portafilters into the groups but make sure you do not tighten them too much in order not to damage the gaskets.
- Remove the drip tray and wash it with water and detergent – the grids can be washed in the cup washer.
- Clean the chassis with a dump cloth e special detergent.
- Clean the steam wands, applying specific procedures and products.

Customer service

Side.
A different cloth should be used for each cleaning function – they should be easily identifiable and always in their place. In the picture, for example, the dump red cloth is for cleaning the steam wand, the blue one is for the drip tray grid and the dry brown one for filters and spout

Service is an essential, yet delicate issue for the Barista. There are several different ways to offer a proper service to customers and sometimes you need to be flexible to adapt to the different types of customers.
Obviously, the Barista will have to follow the dispositions of the coffeehouse manager and should not evaluate these elements on their own.
However, there are some universal, essential principles that the Barista can stick to.

First, creating a cosy atmosphere where the customer can feel welcome and accepted – trying to see the service from the customer's point of view.

Giving attention
The first form of hospitality is giving attention to your guests. Looking at them in the eyes and devoting all the time that is necessary to understand their needs without preconceptions and without taking for granted that you already know what they want.

Customised service
Once you have understood the customer's needs, suggest the products that best meet their specific needs among the products available at your coffeehouse.

Understanding needs
With passing customers or during certain work hours (breakfast), a quick service is certainly a sign of professionalism, since the commitment to quality will not affect the time available to the customer.

Developing intuition
Once you have established a connection with the customer, try to understand which product can best meet their needs despite what they have actually asked for. This way, you will go beyond a mere reactive service, and propose products or services that the customer did not even imagine they desired.

Before work, you should equip your workstation with all the aids that will let you work efficiently, hygienically and safely.

After these preliminary phases, it is time for action.
A good welcome now consists in devoting your attention to drink preparation.

Precision, cleanness and measured movements are a sign of professionalism and good service.

At the right time and in the right work hour, you might give information on the products used, their origins and processing when serving the drinks, as well as promote the work of those who preceded you in the quality supply chain to convey competence and make the customer perceive quality. Of course, you should pay attention not to penalise the other customers in terms of attention and service.

Cleaning the equipment must be a daily, constant practice for the Barista.

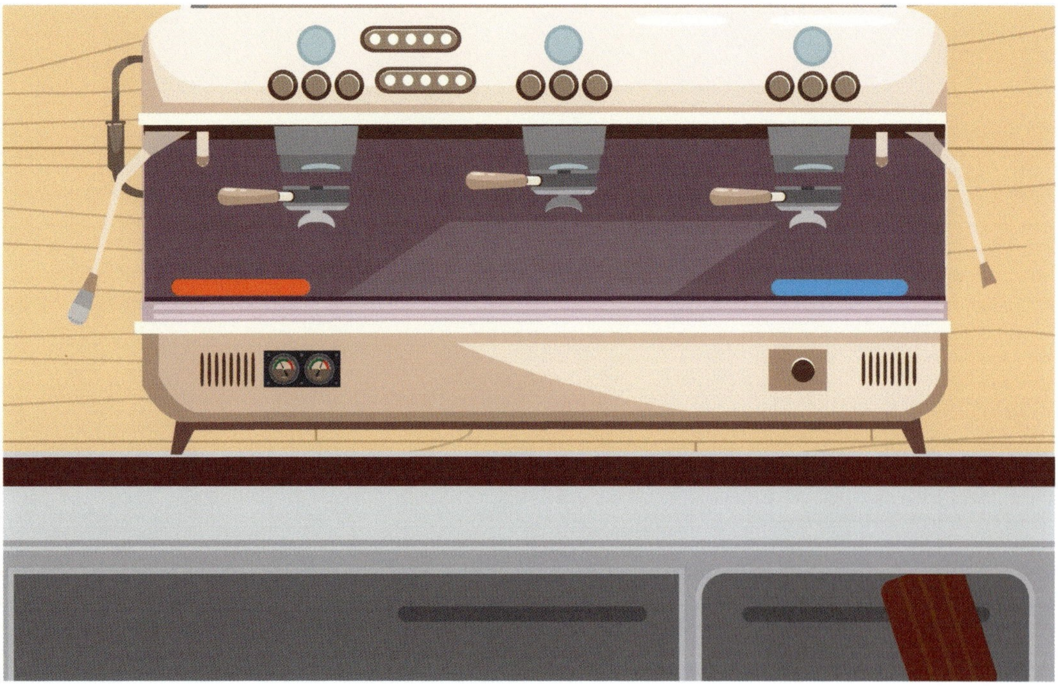

BASIC PRINCIPLES

1. Remember to wear clean, freshly washed clothes
2. Remember to wash your hands frequently
3. Be careful about the danger of burns when you handle hot liquids
4. Always mark and separate toxic substances

Carefully read the instruction provided by the producer when using chemical products.

Hygiene and order

We have already seen the effects of exposing the oils in coffee to environmental agents. Each surface touching the coffee ends up coated with a film of oil, which must be removed constantly to avoid negative sensory effects.

You must take great care and attention in keeping order and hygiene during your work, since they have two essential functions.

The first is purely functional – in a tidy place, work flows more smoothly, tools are always in place and you can make measured, precise movements automatically, 'with your eyes closed', with great benefits in terms of efficiency and calmness.

Cleanliness provides you with perfectly efficient equipment, accessible work surfaces and intact ingredients. The second function is communicative.
Order and cleanliness communicate attention and devotion to work, make the customer trust the management, reassure them about any potential safety/hygiene risks linked to the activity of serving food and drinks and make them relax and devote their attention to choosing the products.

The perception of a clean, tidy environment starts from the Baristas, who must have a pleasant look.

Their clothes – including the aprons – must be clean, pleasant, appropriate and freshly washed. A pleasant haircut/hairdo also conveys a nice and clean image.

Hands deserve particular care, since they are the main tools used for preparing the recipes.

It is recommended that the Barista is as neutral as possible also in their 'personal smells', so they can use neutral deodorants and avoid too strong perfumes.

A dedicated towel for the hands and one other for the cups are also needed.

The Barista must pay attention to their nutrition as well; garlic and onion can release unpleasant smells for a long time, so we recommend that you avoid eating them before work. The same is true for cigarettes.

Before starting work, set all the necessary tools out on the workstation for a hygienic, safe and efficient work. Make sure that the equipment – particularly the electrical devices – is perfectly clean and efficient, that the parameters for preparing the recipes are respected and that there are no anomalies that can compromise the Barista's safety and health. A tamper needs to be positioned in a place that is handy for the Barista but is not reached by steam and liquids.

A dry cloth for filter cleaning, a dump cloth for steam wand cleaning, a cloth for cleaning the drip tray grid and one or more cloths for cleaning work surfaces must also be at hand.

A towel for the hands and a towel for the pottery are also needed. Each of them must be easily identifiable and distinguishable by colour and/or dimensions.

First, when you get to the workstation, you need to wash and rinse your hands accurately.

This simple action prevents many hygiene-health problems, so we suggest that you repeat it regularly during your worktime.

Be very careful not to get burnt when using the espresso machine – water, steam and some parts of the machine are very hot and can cause severe burns.

You must pay great attention also when you handle and serve the hot drinks to preserve your and your customers 'safety.

Unfortunately, when Baristas handle the pottery during drink brewing, they often grab the cups by their rims, which later will be touched by the customers 'lips, or even put their fingers inside the cups to take them from the cup warming tray.

This is unhygienic and disgusting to see, and must be avoided.

When you use milk, make sure it does not spill out from its vessels. Remove any possible splashes with an appropriate cloth.

Remember to clean the external part of the steam wand after every use and its internal part by purging and removing any drop from the jet with the appropriate cloth.

During equipment cleaning and maintenance, pay attention to hot and moving parts.

You must be appropriately informed also when using chemical products, so please read the producer's instructions carefully and be trained on their use by expert professionals before using them.

Always wash your hands at the beginning and frequently during your work shift.

Coffee

ARABICA

Coffea arabica is a species of Coffea. It was the first species to be cultivated, and currently represents approximately 60% of global production.

Arabica originates from Ethiopia, where it grows spontaneously. It was introduced and planted in Yemen, and from this land, was gradually transported to many countries for cultivation. Brazil is the world's largest Arabica producer. The beautiful and glossy leaves are dark green, the flowers are white, with an incredible fragrance that resembles the sweet smell of jasmine flowers.

The seeds are contained in a drupe (commonly called a "cherry"), 10–15 mm in diameter. Mature drupe can be red, yellow, or orange in colour, and typically contains two seeds, the actual coffee beans.

Sometimes there is only one seed inside the drupe, and this is called a Peaberry.

The plants need approximately 5 or more years to mature fully, and they are fragile and vulnerable to parasites and fungal infections.

Arabica is usually cultivated from 900 to 2,000 metres (or higher) above sea level (3,000 - 6,600 Ft).

The plant can tolerate low temperatures, but not frost, and it does best with an average temperature between 15 and 25 °C (60-80 °F).

Plants are frequently trimmed as low as 2 m to facilitate either mechanical or manual harvesting. Because all cherries do not ripen at the same time, only manual harvesting (or "picking"), is capable of selecting only the ripe cherries, and this produces better quality coffee.

AROMA

Green coffee beans do not have much aroma. It's only through roasting that we create the various volatile compounds that make coffee aroma.

The complexity of aromas relies on the composition of chemical compounds in the green beans.

Their presence depends on many variables, including variety, weather conditions, level of maturation, and processing after harvesting.

CAFFEINE

This is the coffee plant's natural defence against parasites. Arabica ranges from 0,8 - 1,4% caffeine, and Robusta (Coffea Canephora) from 1,7 - 4% caffeine.

It is found throughout the coffee plant but is more concentrated in the seed / coffee bean.

Caffeine is a bitter tasting compound, highly soluble in water, and has a physiological effect on humans.

CARBON DIOXIDE

Degassing is the release of gases from roasted coffee. When you roast coffee, gases – mostly carbon dioxide – form inside the bean.

A lot of these gases are released in the first few days after roasting, so a short period of degassing is recommended before extracting espresso.

In other words, if you brew coffee too freshly roasted, it can negatively affect the flavour profile of the coffee, and you can find many bubbles on your espresso crema.

CHANNELLING
When high-pressure water is forced into the espresso puck, the water finds the path of least resistance through the puck.

If the coffee is not distributed evenly, the water may find a specific narrow path through the puck, instead of flowing through the entire puck evenly.

Channeling causes over and under extraction of different areas of the puck. The result is a shot with muddied, unclear flavours, or a generally under-extracted cup.

COFFEA
Coffea is a genus of flowering plants in the Rubiacee family: there are over 120 species of Coffea. The two most popular are Coffea Arabica (commonly known simply as "Arabica"), and Coffea Canephora (known as "Robusta").

CREMA
Crema is a foam, principally composed of carbon dioxide contained in emulsified oils, both of which have been forced out of the coffee grounds by the high pressure water during espresso extraction.

It ranges in different color from blond to reddish-brown or dark brown. A pale crema may be evidence of under-extraction or old coffee, while dark brown or black crema may be evidence of over-extraction or an overly hot boiler.

DRUPE
Drupe: this is the coffee berry. Coffee is a stone fruit and it looks very similar to a cherry.

What we commonly call a "coffee bean" is actually one of the two seeds contained inside the fruit of the plant. Coffee beans are seeds of the coffee plant.

FLAVOUR

When we perceive a flavour, it is often actually aroma. In fact our tongue perceives only mouthfeel and sweet, salty, bitter, and sour tastes. When these tastes combine with the aroma sensed by receptors in the nose, we get flavour.

OXIDATION

Generally, exposure of coffee beans to oxygen can cause aroma loss and aromatic degradation.
The oxidation of the coffee oil, naturally present in the roasted coffee bean, produces rancid tastes.

If there is oil migration to the bean surface, these effects occur quickly, and are very unpleasant. This is one of the reasons why hoppers must be cleaned daily.

ROASTING

Roasting coffee transforms the chemical and physical properties of green coffee beans into roasted coffee products.

The roasting process causes many chemical reactions that produce the characteristic flavour of coffee. Simply changing the roasting intensity from light to dark can produce significantly different flavours in the cup from the same green coffee.

ROBUSTA

Robusta is a species of Coffea. Though widely known as Robusta, it's correct name is Coffea Canephora.

Robusta it is less susceptible to pests and disease than Arabica, because it contains more caffeine - a chemical defence produced by the plants themselves.

Robusta originates from Western and Central Africa. Nowadays, Vietnam is the world's greatest producer of Robusta.

Robusta is easier to care for and has a greater crop yield than Coffea Arabica, so it is cheaper to produce.

Plants grow up to 10-12 m (33-40 Ft.) . There are typically two seeds contained in the drupe, but they are almost always smaller than those of the Arabica species. Robusta plants can tolerate temperatures sustained between 20 and 30°C. (70-85°F).

Roasted robusta beans produce a strong, full-bodied coffee with a distinctive earthy flavour, usually with more bitterness than Arabica. Good-quality robusta beans are sometimes used in espresso blends, to provide a full-bodied taste and thick crema, to suit the taste preferences and local coffee culture in some countries.

ESPRESSO MACHINE

FILTER BASKET

The filter basket is the filter container for the ground coffee dose. It is produced in stainless steel and has holes in the bottom that allow the liquid loaded with the substances solubilised from the coffee to pass, but retain most of the insoluble fibres.

Filter baskets are produced in different sizes and shapes. In the upper part of the wall there is, in most filters, a recess around the circumference where the spring is inserted.

GROUP DISPENSE SWITCH

This is a button, small lever or paddle in espresso machines that operates the pump and simultaneously provides the impulse that opens the solenoid valve. This allows the flow of water towards the coffee puck.

GROUP DOSING KEYPAD

The automatic and super-automatic espresso machines offer, through the keypad, the possibility of programming the volume of water to be dispensed. Delivery is then automatically stopped once the set volume is dispensed.

GROUP GASKET

The group gasket is a flexible O-ring with a diameter that matches that of the filter.

When the filter holder is inserted into the group, the edge of the filter comes into contact with the gasket and seals the system. It is housed inside a groove made in the filter holder disc. Due to the frictional wear, and hardening caused by intense heat, the gasket needs to be replaced periodically.

GROUP HEAD

The group is the point of the espresso machine from which the water from the boiler comes out, to prepare the espresso.

The group conveys the water to a permeable metal disc that disperses the jet, and is at the center of a bayonet coupling system where the filter holder is secured.

On the outside of the disc there is a rubber gasket which, once coupled with the edge of the filter, ensures the closure of the system, allowing the internal pressure to rise.

Professional machines usually have more than one group, and some have a boiler for each group and are called multiple or multi-boiler boiler. In multi boiler machines it is possible to set different and independent temperatures for each group.

HOT WATER TAP

Provides hot water from the steam boiler.
In some machines, it is possible to mix boiler water with cold water to adjust the water temperature as desired.

PORTAFILTER HOLDER

Contains the filter, and conveys the beverage to the cups via the spouts. It is usually manufactured from chromed brass or stainless steel.

It is equipped with lateral bayonet coupling segments, which match with the assembly coupling guides. It has a handle, usually made of plastic or wood, which acts as a handle and lever to release and lock the filter holder to the group with little effort. Some filter holders are without the lower cup and spouts, leaving the bottom of the filter bare. This is why they are called Naked (Bottomless).

PRESSURE GAUGE

The pressure gauge is usually located on the front of the machine and indicates the boiler pressure and the pump operating pressure; two very important parameters for espresso brewing and for frothing milk.

The temperature is directly proportional to the pressure, therefore, the water temperature can be obtained from the pressure value in the steam boiler.

SHOWER SCREEN

The shower screen is also located in the group. It is sometimes referred to as a dispersion screen, shower screen or shower.

It is a perforated metal screen with a diameter smaller than that of the filter. It acts as a diffuser for the water flow from the group before it reaches the coffee cake. Without this device, the concentrated jet of water would damage the coffee cake.

SPRING

The spring holds the filter basket in place. It is held in the portafilter by clipping into a groove that is milled into the inner surface of the portafilter body.

Some springs are round in profile and circumference, but most are bent into a hexagonal shape with one open end.

STEAM TIP (STEAM WAND TIP)
The steam tip is the terminal of the steam wand. Its purpose is to divide the flow of steam into calibrated, ordered and angled flows to allow ideal and uniform steaming of the milk.

Espresso machine manufacturers often offer a range of steam tips to meet the preferences of Baristas.

STEAM WAND
This is a metal tube that delivers the steam from the steam boiler. It is the device used to heat and froth milk.

GRINDERS

ADJUSTMENT RING OR KNOB

This grinder component allows you to change the size of the coffee grounds, making the grinds coarser or finer. The adjustment ring or knob is usually found below the bean hopper.

BEAN HOPPER

This is a container, usually with a cone-like shape, which acts as a feeding tank for the grinding chamber of the coffee grinder.

Typically manufactured from polycarbonate, it is usually tapered in the lower part to provide consistent feeding into the grinding chamber. It has a lid on top, and a gate in the bottom to open or close feeding to the grinder.

BURRS

There are two types of burrs for non-industrial professional use.

FLAT BURRS: are a pair of circular metal or ceramic discs. One side of each disc is flat, and the other side of each disc has a notched cutting surface. The upper burr is attached to a carrier screwed into the body of the coffee grinder and remains stationary during grinding. The lower burr is attached to the motor shaft and rotates on its axis. The grind size can be varied by rotating the carrier, and changing the distance between the upper and lower burrs.

CONICAL BURRS: the upper fixed burr is a thick crown, with the cutting edge milled on the internal surface. The lower burr, which rotates on the motor axis, is a truncated cone, with the cutting edges milled on the external surface. The lower cone fits within the inside of the upper cone.

DOSER grinder

The dosing mechanism is a volumetric dosing device. It consists of a separator which divides the lower part of the dosing container into wedge portions.

It is equipped with a plate whose height can be varied by turning an adjustment screw. By adjusting the height of the plate, the volume of the segments, and therefore the dose of ground coffee contained in them, are changed.

GRINDER ON DEMAND

On-demand grinders are not equipped with a dosing chamber. Ground coffee from on-demand grinders falls from the grinding chamber directly into the filter. The dosage is controlled by a timer that can be adjusted.

By grinding for more or less time, a higher or lower dose is obtained.